DEDICATION

- To my family who agreed Aston Gardens was the best place for me to be in my old age.

- To Jack who added sparkle in my years at Aston Gardens.

- To Jackie who came for coffee so many mornings and let me talk of everything in my life, and who read and criticized my book manuscript – gently!

- To Deirdre who helped me so much with the manuscript and my computer skills

Some of the Resident Occupations in the Past

Horticulturist

Pharmacist

Musician

Minister

Policeman

Plumber

Artist

Actress and Actor

Photographer

Airline Pilot

Landscaper

Astrologist

Veterinarian

Mechanic

Librarian

Dentist

Doctor

Electrician

Baker

Shoemaker

Mailman

COME HOME TO ASTON

BARBARA MALTBY

outskirtspress

DENVER, COLORADO

PREFACE

My idea to write a book about Aston Gardens came during my first occupancy there from 2005 to 2009. I made lots of notes about the interesting people and happenings and saved all the monthly copies of *What's Up*, a newsletter which told of newcomers, meetings and activities.

I thought it would be interesting for readers to know the intimate details of an old lady living in one of the Independent Living Facilities. I planned on "***telling it like it is***".

My granddaughter, Windy came to live with me as she wanted to attend college and needed my help in attaining her life goals. The extra costs were too much for my budget, so after living in Aston Gardens for three years, we bought a house in Sun City Center and moved. Windy and I lived there for five years. There I became too busy with house and yard to think much about writing my book, but I saved all my notes.

When I returned to Aston Gardens in 2014 I brought with me a box of paper memories and a renewed interest in writing my book. By now, at age eighty-nine, I had developed physical problems that prohibited long sessions of just sitting and writing so it was all a slow process. As the months passed and I was not "getting any younger" as the saying goes, I felt an urgency to finish the book. By now I had told all my family, friends, dinner companions or the person who sat next to me on the bus that I was writing a book about Aston Gardens. So there was no stopping me, and I wanted to do it for other aging people so they could decide if a place like Aston Gardens might be right for them.

TABLE OF CONTENTS

HISTORY OF
ASTON GARDENS

In May of 1990, Aston Gardens was built by a group of men under the name of Aston Care Systems. They built the Courtyards first and then Aston Gardens. By May of 1999, the first three buildings, three, four and five, were ready for occupancy. A time capsule was buried in front of the clubhouse to mark that event. It was to be dug up in ten years.

An article was printed in *What's Up,* an Aston Gardens newsletter, describing the early days at Aston Gardens. There was only one road at that time for both in and out traffic. New residents were assigned a moving day. Their moving van had to back out after unloading as only one van was allowed in at a time.

Several things happened those first years to make me realize that democracy does work and the elderly can speak up and be listened to. In the spring of 2006 at a monthly business meeting, the Vice President of Operations for Aston Care System (the management team) talked of a new development called Portofina, to be built in Veterans Park, the open grassy area in back of the Clubhouse. Plans were being made for twenty-four two-story villas. Construction was to begin in May and would take about a year. We were told that twenty to twenty-seven existing parking spaces would be lost. They would need to transport workers from a central location to Aston Gardens. A high plastic fence would surround the site. The Vice President also told the residents there would still be a sidewalk around the new buildings and he planned on building a tiki bar, a bocci court and a putting green. We wondered if he was trying to placate the residents, especially after he said that ninety-five trees would need to be relocated.

Residents began to protest these new plans. The editor of *What's Up*, had this to say in the February/March 2006 issue: *"Following discussion regarding Aston's announcement of their plans to build townhouses on the center portion of Aston Gardens North campus, a near unanimous show of hands by those residents attending the monthly business breakfast on February 17, 2006 supported an urgent request that Aston management delay proceeding with the project because of its negative impact on current residents with no offsetting positive aspects. If management believes it needs an additional source of reliable income, while at the same time offering potential tangible benefits to many current and future residents, then we urge objective consideration of building a single story residence to accommodate those who may require assisted living or memory care services, with Aston Gardens residents having first priority."*

Another personal response from this Editor said, *"What! You say that we are going to lose our park! That can't be true! Back in the spring of 1999 when my husband and I were considering selling our home and moving into a retirement facility, we decided on Aston Gardens because we were told that the park would belong to the residents and that either a shuffleboard court or a miniature golf course would be placed there. We were so thrilled by the whole concept, that we made a donation to help pay for the fish pond and on November 11, 2001 the park was dedicated to veterans and named Veterans Park. Although the sports elements never came to fruition, benches were added and walking areas built, trees and plants added and it became a beautiful place to walk and relax. Taking back the park would have been an insult to the residents and a slap in the face to veterans."*

Another resident of Aston Gardens wrote a long letter to the President of Aston Care Systems, Inc. on February 14, 2006 which said:

"My wife and I moved to Aston Gardens North in July, 2005, after spending the better part of a year researching other un-assisted living facilities in Florida. Our initial visit here in May, 2004, and our second visit in May, 2005 resulted in signing the deposit paperwork. We also visited your Parkland facility. Until last month we felt we had made the right decision.

"Our primary reason for deciding to sell our home and move to an un-assisted living community was to relieve our five children from the trauma of finding suitable care for Mom and Dad when one or the other survived, but was then unable to care for her/himself without assistance. Here, we were lead to believe, we would have first priority for accommodations at either assisted living or memory care at the Courtyards, until a similar facility was built in the center of our campus.

"Since hearing of your announcement last month to erect townhouses instead, we have been terribly disappointed. Our conversations with a number of other residents, including some

who have been here since the beginning, support our disbelief. I suspect we now recognize a pattern of your financial personnel controlling the operations people to continually downsize the expense budget (services and food, for example). Achieving essentially 100% occupancy has apparently resulted in a corporate mantra of 'Let's get all we can, right now!

"Our age group does not like surprises. We want stability and consideration, especially when we're paying a substantial monthly rent, and a sincere and supportive staff of service providers. We recognize that profit oriented corporations need to reward their shareholders with a stream of profit oriented. Yet we are also hopeful, we trust not naively, that corporations invested in the senior care field will have a corporate culture that resists the urge to milk it for all they can.

"Should you decide to continue with your current plans, with the downside for current residents noted above, plus subjecting us to all the noise and dust (including our cars) and pollution attendant to a long period of construction; and the significant loss of parking spaces and greenery and unobstructed views from apartments facing onto the commons, and further demands on the dining room/kitchen staff and seating, then it is reasonable to expect that you will compensate us for interfering with the right to enjoyment of our premises, as provided by our leases.

"When I was a CEO it was corporate policy that the 'bean counters' and lawyers did not have responsibility for running the company; the operations executives and managers did. We also insisted that we were in business to serve our customers best interests."

There were many discussions between the management team of Aston Care Systems, and the residents. The residents composed a letter "To The Editor" and it was published in newspapers in the area with a copy to the Chairman of the Board of Aston Care Systems.

Assistance was also required from the County Office of Rhonda Storm, Hillsborough County Commission, the Department of Aging and the Planning Department. Petitions were signed and the uproar against Portofino was loud and relentless.

A final response from the management team said: *"In an effort to more fully understand the needs, cares, and concerns of residents at Aston Gardens North, Aston Care Systems has decided to hold progress on our planned new community of villas known as Portofino. This action is in response to our management team having met individually with several residents who have expressed their thoughtful concern."* And further: *"We will now embark on another evaluation of the use of our land. This evaluation will once again take into consideration the opinions, thoughts and concerns of you, our valued resident. The final decision will be a "new" reflection of your input, together with our vision for the overall campus."*

So the years slipped by and Portofino was not mentioned again, nor was there any plans made for Assisted Living in Veterans Park. Residents and wildlife continue to enjoy the walking paths, koi pond, and special plantings.

Soon after the Portofino problem Aston Gardens was sold to Sunrise Senior Living, a Washington, D. C. based company with headquarters in McLean, Virginia. Sunrise offered a variety of senior living services in more than four hundred twenty communities in thirty-eight states and four countries including Canada, United Kingdom, Germany, and the United States. This company vowed to be continually dedicated to "Champion quality of life for seniors" by: encouraging independence, enabling choice, preserving dignity, celebrating individuality, nurturing the spirit and involving family and friends.

During the ownership of Aston Gardens by Sunrise, the Executive Director distributed an "Executive Director Update" on a regular basis telling what was being done at Aston Gardens and about any changes. Due to a difference of opinion about the operation of the Activities Department the Executive Director decided to fire Susanne who was head of that department.

Meanwhile the residents were beginning to object to losing Susanne who was an excellent Activities Director, and had worked hard at Aston Gardens from the beginning. So petitions were again circulated and signed to get our Susanne back.

I do not know about the inner workings of management or what happened behind closed doors at Aston, but before too long we had a new Executive Director and one of her first projects was to bring Susanne home to Aston to work again with so many who loved her. She planned a Welcome Party in the ballroom and the place was packed with residents who gave Susanne a standing ovation This was another time we did see democracy work well.

In 2009 Aston Gardens was sold again and Discovery Management was in charge. Plans for the future included a desire to return to a gourmet level of food and to have a "rent protection plan" so that the rates could be locked in for three years.

Today Discovery Management still manages Aston Gardens and does a good job, in my opinion. Many of us elders can have our meals served in a Country Club setting, live in an apartment with service or help just a phone call or the pull of a cord away, and we can be transported to the Club House, doctor's appointments or other nearby places. It can't get much better than this.

And, by the way, that time capsule that was buried in 1999 when Aston Gardens was built was opened in 2010. Inside was a damp mess of ruined papers. So they buried a more substantial capsule to be opened in another ten years. I may not be around to see the contents, but then I am not sure I care!

WHAT DO I DO NOW?

CHAPTER 1

The funeral of my husband, Gordon, my partner for six-ty-four years, was over. I wanted company to help silence the cries of loneliness, but most of all I wanted to have fun in my life again. There was no laughter. I used to say that life was not worth living without laughter—lots of it. I read that laughter is a tranquilizer with no side effects. There did not seem to be enough reasons to go on. There would be no more traveling with recreational vehicles, going west each summer, camping in the wilderness and listening to the night noises. No one was there to hold me at night. I could feel a case of self-pity developing and I would need to make efforts to change this depressing outlook. Family and friends could help, but it would be me who needed to take action.

My oldest son, David, wanted to help bring back the ex-citement of life for me so asked me to join his family on a cruise to Alaska—my favorite state. There I found beauty, awesome glaciers and interesting people, but somehow it was not the same without Gordon.

Then David took me to Las Vegas hoping the lights and glitter and excitement of this place would spark interest in me to "get back into life". When I returned home from this second trip I was ready to make changes, take chances and look for purpose in my life. I took a test given by Eric Butterworth, a spiritual writer, to find out whether my mission on earth was finished. The results of the test were that if I am alive, it isn't.

I made a list of Independent Living facilities around Sun City Center that might be right for me. The list included Freedom Plaza, Sun Towers, The Courtyards and Aston Gardens. Freedom Plaza required you buy your apartment and I wanted to rent; and besides there were so many dining rooms that it might be difficult to develop friendships. Freedom Plaza had lifetime care and I was not ready to look that far ahead. Sun Towers was considered a high-rise compared to the mostly one and two story homes and other buildings in the area. It seemed more like an institution rather than a home. Courtyards was nice but showed signs of age (like me) and although near a shopping center, it just did not have appeal for me.

The final stop I made in my hunt for independent living quarters, was at Aston Gardens. Son, David joined me for a tour. We found the entrance road where East Del Web meets West Del Web and drove down a winding road with signs on each side. One sign read, "Welcome Home to Aston", and another said, "3 Years Guaranteed Rental". On the other side of the road, so you could read it leaving Aston Gardens, the sign read, "Come Home to Aston". We passed a lake on each side of the road and there were several large alligators sunning themselves on the grassy bank nearby. After passing an empty sentry stand, we came to Aston Gardens. The Clubhouse had stately columns in front and a clock tower on the top of the building with a weather vane on top of that.

We walked past manicured shrubs and big urns and the place where we heard a time capsule had been buried when Aston Gardens was built in 1999, not to be dug up for ten years. As I entered the Clubhouse I wondered if this could be my last place to call home.

We met our rental agent, who told us there were ten apartment buildings that encircled the Clubhouse. Each apartment building had an entrance into a foyer where there was a bathroom, mail boxes for the residents, and a bulletin board for notices about activities. In the bathroom there was a shopping cart for the use of the tenants for groceries, luggage or other things. There was a card room on the second floor with two card tables, eight chairs, several lounge chairs and a sink with counter and cabinets. Each apartment had a small shelf by the door so timely items for special occasions or interests of the tenant could be displayed.

There was a variety of styles for apartments from the Canterbury with one bedroom, one bath, kitchen and living area, to the very large Harrington with two bedrooms, 2½ baths, den, kitchen, dining area, and living room.

We then had a tour of the Clubhouse with an in-depth explanation of the use of each particular room. When we entered the lobby on the left was the library operated by volunteer residents. Books are acquired by donation, but with so many moving in and feeling the need to downsize, there was a never ending supply of books. Readers did not need to sign out books. There were labels on each shelf for all types of reading material like autobiographies, biographies, medical, religious, health and others. There were both paperbacks and hard cover books with some in large print. A magazine rack was on the wall and on the table were several newspapers like the Wall Street Journal, Tampa Tribune and Observer. By the front window there were all kinds of dictionaries, Sun City Center and Tampa phone books, a list of the residents and a telephone for local use.

In the attached computer room were four computers and a printer for resident use. There was also another cabinet there for books on the history of our country and other countries.

When we returned to the lobby we decided to relax by sitting on the comfortable chairs and a couch, enjoying the huge fireplace and listening to the grand piano music. Then we checked the table to see if there were any red roses in vases often placed there when a resident dies, with a photo and information about any memorial service. We were told that this lobby is decorated for all special holidays.

We stopped at the Concierge Desk where one can do many things; like ask questions, pick up the menu for the week, drop off the rent check, ask for a work order to fix something in your apartment, request a ride to a doctor appointment or back to your apartment, buy stamps, fax papers, mail packages, send out dry cleaning, or check the lost and found items.

In the lobby are several boxes; one for suggestions or complaints and another box to put in your monthly or yearly tips for the Employee Appreciation Fund. There has always been a no tipping rule at Aston Gardens but the residents felt the faithful service of the hourly employees should be rewarded, so the Employee Appreciation Fund was established in 1999. Contributions were voluntary and could be made during the year and would be distributed in December of each year.

Walking to the right, down a hall, you would first see the special dining room that could seat up to ten persons for special parties held by residents. The offices of the management of Aston Gardens were further down this hall. Across from the offices were many sign-up sheets for activities including the Monday bridge game, bus trips and other activities.

Off the main lobby was the spacious, attractive dining room with its huge chandeliers and fresh flowers on the tables. By this time I was feeling very much at home and loving the place. David and I were seated for a delicious lunch and a chance to talk things over before finishing our tour.

After lunch we walked down the main hall. On the left was a room for employees and on the right was the lounge and bar where you could get a cocktail, beer or soft drinks. We were told there was always a special drink of the day for two dollars. The price was right. The bartender also played games with the patrons with free drinks as prizes for the winners.

Beyond the bar and part of the lounge was a special place called the Cozy Corner. This area could be used at cocktail hour for the patrons of the bar, a bridge game, or a place during the day to have coffee with a friend. There was always a table nearby with coffee, juice, water, fruit and cookies available for everyone.

Next was the Billiard room, which had been designed in quite a sophisticated manner. There you could shoot a game of pool, play darts, have a poker game or play bridge.

The spacious ballroom was near the end of the hall and used for many activities. It had a stage, seating for a large crowd and was used for plays, parties, movies (even had a popcorn machine), meetings, dances, lectures, exercise classes, bingo, bridge games and church services on Sunday.

Activities Director, Susanne's office was next to the ballroom, and across the hall from a glass enclosure for displaying interests or hobbies of the residents. Nearby was an activity room for games, puzzles and storage.

Across the hall was the Doctor/Nurse station. The occupancy of this room would change over time and provide a variety of health care by a resident doctor or nurse.

The workout room nearby had treadmills, weights for lifting, and other equipment to build strength and muscles.

The next room was the beauty parlor. Here you could get your hair cut, permed, or dyed and your nails done. We heard that no one left this salon without a hug. It was also the main setting for Aston Garden's gossip.

Outside the back door at this end was the pool and hot tub and many lounges, tables and umbrellas.

Beyond the pool was a large grassy area called Veterans Park, encircled by a cement walking path where there were many trees and shrubs (many with labels) along the way, and a gazebo and koi pond in the middle where one could sit and rest or think. An interesting fact of note is that a walk seven times around this area would equal a mile.

At the end of our tour two things happened. I decided to make Aston Gardens my new home, and I signed the papers and paid my first month rent. After seeing several apartments and with David's urging I got a large place. I chose Building 8 and the large Harrington apartment floor plan on the second floor overlooking the golf course and woods. With the help of family and friends I moved from the duplex in Kings Point to Aston Gardens. I was home.

LIFE BEGINS AT ASTON GARDENS

CHAPTER 2

One of the first things I did after getting settled in my apartment at Aston Gardens was to go to CARE (an animal rescue facility) and adopt a kitten named Tory. I wanted a pet to keep me company, and when I looked through the window of the "kitten room" Tory was pacing back and forth trying to get my attention and seemed to beg me to take her home. It was a good decision as Tory filled a need in my life.

I was very tired that first night and I fell into bed about midnight. Soon the doorbell rang and I went to the door and called, "Who is there?" The answer was, "Security". When I let him in he said my alarm had sounded. In the bathroom and bedroom there are alarm boxes with long cords, and if pulled will alert the office in the Clubhouse that I need help. I explained that I did not need help, just needed sleep, and did not pull the cord. So Security left. In about an hour as I was drifting back to sleep, Security rang the bell again. When he came in we both looked down at a very playful kitten named Tory and knew what the problem was. I wound up the cords around the boxes and could never leave them dangling during the rest of my stay.

About the second thing that happened to me after my move was falling and breaking my arm. Just one little mis-step and down I went. Fortunately there were friends with me to help. It did not require a cast, just a sling, and my arm healed in several weeks.

Another small incident involving Tory again happened. I shut the front door and heard a loud yowl from a very upset cat. When I opened the door, Tory's tail had a definite bend near the end which from then on caused guilt feelings for me when I looked at it, as I was the one who shut the door on her tail.

One thing that attracted me to Aston Gardens was that everything was so close and I could just walk across the street from my building to the Clubhouse. I began to attend exer-cise classes like Yoga, The Art of Tai Chi, Smiling Yoga for the Face (that was a unique one), a balance evaluation (I learned I had little balance), walked with the Sunshine Walkers, swam during the pool exercises and attended a needed Eat Better and Move More class.

Since bridge was my favorite game and good for improv-ing the mind, I joined the Monday afternoon Duplicate group. I found many private bridge games being played in individual apartments, in the Cozy Corner, or in a corner of the Billiards Room, and I was asked to be a substitute many times. Later I would take bridge lessons and play at the Atrium building in Sun City Center.

There were many other games offered at the Clubhouse, like Bingo, Whist, Mahjongg, Hand and Foot, Billiards and others.

Shopping was another favorite activity at Aston Gardens.

At times an "Aston Mall" would be held in the lobby with vendors such as Mary Kaye, Avon or jewelry sales. A White Elephant Exchange Party was held in the Clubhouse so residents could get rid of things too good to throw away and acquire more things they would eventually throw away.

You could join a Travel Club and go on exciting cruises. Movies were shown each Saturday night and Sunday afternoon. I had to chuckle one time when we all got a memorandum saying, "The movie, Under the Stars, will be postponed until a later day because tomorrow's forecast is predicting rain."

A very interesting serious of lectures had been given since Sunrise was the owner and is still being provided twice a month. Professor Philip Leto is the orator for the Sterling University Lectures about a variety of unusual subjects starting with, "The Road to The White House". In a welcome letter to Aston Gardens residents, Philip Leto said, "Some believe that as an individual ages, intellectual curiosity and the desire to learn is somehow diminished. Our experience shows otherwise. We find successful retirees to be among the most intellectually curious and knowledgeable learners we have encountered. Sterling University was developed to feed your yearning for knowledge in a manner that recognizes that you are highly informed learners. We understand that tapping the reservoirs of your personal experience is vital to the success of each class session. Through lively, topical and information-packed sessions, we hope to engage you in a 'complete cognitive workout'."

Another letter from Professor Leto said, "We hope you will join us as we embark on the educational journey that has been designed to inform and entertain you while at the same time nurture your healthy, active minds."

A birthday party for all residents is held each month to honor those with birthdays or anniversaries that month. Wine and beer are served with cheese, crackers and fruit. Dance music is provided by a one man band; and it was fun to watch dancers carrying portable oxygen tanks, or those who usually use a cane or walker, cavorting carefully on the dance floor. Then the party goers go to the dining room to feast on a special birthday dinner of surf and turf (lobster and prime ribs), stuffed baked potato, asparagus and birthday cake. Birthday parties are a much loved tradition at Aston Gardens.

Susanne tells a story about the early days of Aston when a man died on the dance floor at one of the birthday parties. After his body was removed by the Emergency Squad some of the residents were ready to return to the dance floor, but Susanne said, "No—time to go home".

Every year special celebrations for special days or holiday times are held at Aston Gardens. There was a Chinese New Year's when we would all get fortune cookies as part of our dessert. At the New Year's Eve party the clocks would be turned back so when we all thought it was midnight and time to celebrate the coming of the New Year, it was actually 10 p.m. Yes, actually somewhere in the world it is midnight. This allowed everyone to feel the excitement of New Year's Eve and yet get to bed at a reasonable hour. The floral arrangements and decorations around the clubhouse indicated whether it was time for Christmas, Easter, July 4th or other celebrations.

In February we all felt love and remembered different times on Valentine's Day that were special. Sometimes Susanne would make a collage of photos of the residents suffering the pangs of young love in their younger years.

We celebrated summer with the annual picnic buffet.

In the fall we experienced Octoberfest with beer and German foods of all kinds.

Christmas was festive with many activities such as carol singing, a trip to Mt. Dora to see the lights, or a holiday boutique expo.

Many special shows would be hosted at Aston like the Classic Car Show, a Pet Promenade with fancy duds on the tenant's pets, or the Hawaiian Luau night with hula dancers in grass skirts.

Sun City Center sponsored the Swim Dancers at the Atrium Lap Pool. We were all invited to watch two of our own residents perform intricate synchronized swimming routines.

Another activity was a tour of the kitchen to see where and how our meals were prepared. One day the kitchen sponsored a "Make it and Take it Candy Day" for the "sweettooths" around Aston.

Many comedy night musical shows and plays kept life interesting for all of us at Aston Gardens.

A very important advantage to life here was that Aston Gardens paid the annual admission fee for all of us to belong to the Sun City Center Recreation Center so we could enjoy the use of the pools, tennis courts, shuffleboard courts, hobbies, 150 clubs, another library, classes, movies, dances and so much more.

In the early days of my rental Lionel was Security and often the driver of the many-seated golf cart that drove residents to and from the buildings and clubhouse. All you had to do was call the front desk and ask to go to the Clubhouse and soon the golf cart would come for you. You could bring your walker with you and the driver of the cart would help you.

We were all given welcome instructions when we moved in. Breakfast was from 7:30 a.m. to 9 a.m. and lunch and dinner between 11:30 a.m. to 6:30 p.m. Sunday would be just brunch from 10:30 a.m to 1:30 p.m. No shorts were allowed after 3 p.m. We were all responsible for taking our trash to the Trash Room available on each floor of each building. Housekeeping would assign each apartment a cleaning day. On that day the housekeeper would also wash bed linens and towels.

Soon I settled down and developed my routine. My day always started with a cup or two of coffee, reading the newspaper delivered to my door, and doing the crossword puzzle. If I had company for dinner we would sit in my apartment at cocktail time in the dusk of early evening. Often bobcats would walk out onto the golf cart paths on the golf course looking for prey such as rabbits, mice, squirrels or even a house cat or two. It added excitement to our "drinking time" and a little shiver too. Now and then we would see a red fox hunting for the same small animals. After dinner I usually returned to my apartment and settled down in my recliner. Now and then the flashing lights of the emergency vehicles would stop in front of my building, and I would wonder who needed help this time, or who died. One should get used to those flashing lights, but no one ever does. When a death is reported or someone has a crippling stroke or breaks bones in a fall, we all secretly wonder if we will be next.

After living in my big apartment for a while, I felt the need to cut my expenses so arranged to move down the hall to a smaller place closer to the elevator. Some said it might have something to do with the fact I had developed gypsy inclinations in my life, moving from place to place—and I just could not stop doing this. My special friend, Phyllis said she was tired of helping me move and hoped I would soon stay put. But she faithfully turned up on moving day to help me with the things the movers would not move. Our first job was a shopping trip to buy a beautiful wooden folding screen to hide the back of my piano when it got to the new location. The store put it in the car, but we had to take it out of the car, up the elevator and to the apartment—a monumental job for two old ladies who were unsteady on their feet. We carried it on the grocery cart, wrestled it in to and out of the elevator causing some damage to the elevator structure. The guilt of causing such damage sent us into gales of giggles.

One day in the early years of my stay at Aston I was on my way to the dining room, feeling strong hunger pangs. As I passed by the men's room in the Clubhouse I heard a call for help—over and over. Several ladies were with me and we had to decide what to do. We could not go into the men's room as we were ladies. We finally asked the first gentleman who happened by to check on the emergency. He soon came out of the bathroom with a strange look on his face and said, "Bob is missing a shoe and won't leave without it." None of it made any sense. Finally Security arrived to help Bob find his shoe and came out of the bathroom with an even stranger look on his face and said, "Bob shit in his shoe." When Housekeeping got Bob's shoe cleaned and the men's room cleaned too, we could all return to normal. I was beginning to wonder just what normal really was.

The most exciting, frightening episode that happened while I lived at Aston Gardens was labeled in one of the local papers as "Just one of those crazy days". It happened in June of 2006. It was the day President Bush flew into Macdill Air Force Base on Air Force One and boarded a helicopter that flew over Aston Gardens going to the Wimama Airport. From there he was taken by motorcade to the King's Point Clubhouse to make a speech, and later to the Club Renaissance in Sun City Center for lunch. Then he went to the new fire station on Route 674 to thank the firemen for putting out a fire near Big Bend Road. But the firemen were busy with a new brush fire brewing nearby on West Del Webb Boulevard.

That same day I was having my piano lesson at my teacher, Lee Crawley's house. She told me she saw news on the television that there were problems with a fire on West Del Webb Boulevard, just south of Aston Gardens. So we stopped the lesson early and I hurried home. When I got to my building, there were County workers there helping Security with the evacuation of Aston Gardens and I was told I must leave. I thought of Tory, my precious cat, so I brushed by the workers saying, "I must get my cat." The elevator was closed so I climbed the stairs, quickly stuffed my cat into the pet carrier and struggled back down the stairs avoiding the residents who had to be helped or carried down the stairs. I then drove to my friend, Phyllis's house to stay during the emergency.

Other residents from Aston Gardens were taken by bus to the Courtyards accompanied by some servers and kitchen staff from Aston Gardens. There they were fed and returned by bus when the emergency was over. Afterward there was some question about whether Aston Gardens should have been evacuated, but with so many residents who needed help, I guess they did not want to take any chances.

The cause of the fire was a possible lightning strike or wires contacting the pole. No one was ever sure exactly what happened.

We were told to be ready for a hurricane or a bad storm during the season that spawned hurricanes. Instructions were to have first aid supplies on hand, some canned foods and water (one gallon per person per day). If we had a bath tub in our apartment we were told to fill it with water. Other items to have on hand included flashlight and batteries, a battery operated radio with extra batteries, a ten day supply of prescription drugs and oxygen if needed. Second floor residents were to find a "buddy" on the first floor where they could stay if needed. Each building had a warden. We were to bring in anything from the patio that could blow around, store valuables and irreplaceable treasures in empty appliances, pack some dry clothing in plastic bags, put plastic bags over televisions, lamps, and computers and to be sure to keep a set of tools handy.

In June of 2007 my granddaughter Windy moved in with me. She needed help in getting on with her life and wanted to return to college. She seemed to love older people and the residents all loved her. The added expenses of having her with me was causing too much strain on my limited income, so the decision was made for me to buy a house and leave Aston Gardens. For the next five years Windy and I lived in Sun City Center in a home on Ojai Avenue. I could not continue with my book, but saved all my notes.

THE SECOND
TIME AROUND

CHAPTER 3

The decision was made finally in 2014 to sell my home and return to Aston Gardens. Windy, my granddaughter, was ready to be on her own and go on with her life—so I was free to go on with mine. I put the house on the market and after it sold, I had a big garage sale, as I had to down-size a lot. So many came to help with the sale and move to Aston. My son Danny came from Colorado to help me with the decisions, financial questions and just moral sup-port from a loved one.

Dan and I walked by the tall pillars and into the lobby of Aston again and it felt like I was coming home. We met a different rental agent this time. He showed us a small one bedroom apartment in Building 6. The previous renter had installed a dark wood laminate flooring in the living room to go with his African motif. I also decorated my living room with African memorabilia so I deemed this to be a sign for me to say, "I'll take this one." And I did.

Dan insisted I needed a battery operated GoGo Cart to go back and forth between the Clubhouse and my building. He felt this would give me a sense of freedom. I felt I had a new toy and loved it. Friends loved to see me flying off in my GoGo Cart.

I noticed several additions or changes when I returned to Aston Gardens. Various televisions were installed throughout the Clubhouse to help residents keep up with the weather updates and activities. The time capsule had been dug up after ten years of burial and the contents had been destroyed by water in the soil and it had to be replanted for another ten years.

The biggest change I noticed was that the Residents Association which included many committees such as the Residential Council Association, Welcome Committee, Housekeeping Committee, Activities Committee and others that had served as "watch dogs" and were used to influence policy at Aston were all gone. Management seemed to want to "rule from the top" and not let the occupants have as much say.

Now there were monthly Town Hall meetings at which time a yummy breakfast was served. Each department head reported any changes and would listen to complaints or compliments from the residents. Maintenance might tell the group when the outside windows in each building would be cleaned or why they were slow getting shrubs trimmed by the apartment buildings. The head of Transportation might explain why all the buses were now painted blue. Susanne, head of Activities would foretell about some interesting shows, ball games or dances in the planning stage.

They also had a New Members Orientation to replace the old Welcome Committee, so the new residents could hear the rules and get answers to any questions about their new life style.

Another change I noticed was that there were no more alligators sunning on the lake bank near the entrance and no bobcat sightings were reported to me, so I had to get excited about the hundreds of geckos crossing the sidewalks and the squirrels coming out to meet me hoping I was the resident who fed them daily even if it was forbidden by the management to do so. Later they had to get rid of a large number of squirrels as they were so drawn to leftover Aston food and would beg from anyone who came into the park.

I did have an encounter with another wild animal that was interesting. I was in the pool with a friend, Jackie, when we heard a splash in the deep end of the pool. We could see an armadillo struggling or swimming or whatever armadillos do when faced with deep water. The creature seemed to be scared and frantic. I took my plastic noodle to try to get him to go to the shallow end of the pool where there were steps for him to climb out. It took a while and all the time Jackie was calling such things as, "Watch out he will bite or scratch you." and "They carry rabies." Or "He is getting madder by the moment, so you better leave him alone." But I could not abandon him. Jackie called Maintenance but all they did was watch my "noodle urging" and soon left to go back to work. Finally the armadillo crawled out of the pool; and while I was breathing a sigh of relief he ran about five feet to the hot tub and jumped in. Now, I knew he would not survive the heat so renewed my efforts to save him. After giving him the "noodle treatment" again he climbed out and started looking for a place to escape. Jackie and I tried to lure him out of the gate, but he resisted and responded with much kicking of the back legs in anger, and snorting. Not much thanks for saving his life! Finally he squeezed through the slats of the fence and raced to freedom at last. We laugh about this all the time.

The Ambassador Club was still active, recruiting new residents with the promise of "big bucks" for each one successfully convinced to sign up to live at Aston Gardens.

There were quite a few people living here who were here when I came the first time so that made me feel more comfortable in my surroundings. I must say, I saw and felt ghosts of some who had died, as I walked the halls.

Tory, my cat seemed happy to be back from the time she jumped out of her cat carrier into the #206 apartment living room. I wondered if she remembered living here generally, or the specific "tail caught in the door" caper. She was now too old to pull the alarm cords as she had done when we were here before, so I could let them dangle. She especially loved the porch where she could sit among my plants watching the activities below. In fact, it brought some excitement into her life as there was an opening in the screen and she could chase wasps, geckos or palmetto bugs, but I called Maintenance quickly to call a halt to that kind of fun. That was another advantage of living here; you could get a work order for any problems in your apartment and even get them to hang pictures or change a light bulb for you.

I loved my apartment and my lifestyle. Too many family members and friends could not stay overnight due to space and lack of beds, and I could take guests to the dining room, and no longer had to cook much at all. I could see what was going on in the parking area or call to friends coming for a visit to let them know where to park. My view also included a beautiful magnolia tree, palm trees and a glimpse into

Veterans Park, so I could watch all the dogs being walked, hear birds call and get a glimpse of the weather.

One day when I returned from the Clubhouse on my GoGo cart the mail person was delivering the mail to our boxes in the entrance foyer. I waited until she was done and she then turned to me and said, "That is all the mail, Mrs. Maltby," and handed me my letters. I asked her how she remembered names and numbers with all the names she would see in a day's work. She said she even remembered when someone was here before. I reminded her that I had been in Aston Gardens about six years before in another building. She then told me what building I lived in and the room number. Amazing!

DINING ROOM STORIES

CHAPTER 4

The dining room at Aston Gardens was a favorite meeting place for the residents. The main reason was because everyone liked to eat, and the chef and kitchen staff made efforts to have good food. The young servers were always so friendly, patient and caring; and believe me, the help at Aston Gardens needed all three virtues considering the attitudes and complaining nature of some who live here. Actually, dining here could be compared to Country Club style dining.

To give the diners a voice, Aston Gardens holds a Food Forum each month so requests can be made to change some of the menu selections, to hear complaints about the way the food was cooked, or to give compliments to the Chef for a job well done. The meeting would end with the Manager telling everyone about the occupancy status of Aston Gardens, if there was a waiting list for residency, any changes made in guest meals, complimenting the staff and all committee heads for doing a good job.

While at Aston Gardens I ate my meals with many different residents. My main reason was to get to know everyone. Table conversations started with the usual questions, "What building do you live in?", "Where are you from?", "How many children, grandchildren, great-grandchildren do you have?" After such conversations then the talk turned to the latest operation, illness or health problems.

Arriving at the dining room I always looked around for familiar faces. Many were strangers, or else I forgot meeting them before. Short term memory problems such as mine fit in well here as so many are affected by it. You can confide in others here and because short term memory is common it is doubtful any secrets will be retold.

It is a changing population here as residents move out to be near family members or go to Assisted Living facilities as their physical problems worsen.

At first the site of all the walkers, canes, wheel chairs and gogo carts made me feel I was in some kind of medical facility, but the fresh flowers on the tables brightened the scene. I heard a committee was formed called, "The Ladies with Flower Power", and they took care of the arrangements. When I returned to Aston Gardens after my five year absence the fresh flowers had turned into artificial arrangements, but they still brightened the atmosphere of the dining room.

One night I was seated with a woman named Betty who had fallen that day. Evidently she could not find the table where she was first seated so wandered around the dining room and asked to sit with me, and I, of course, said yes. During dinner another diner came over to our table and returned Betty's purse and asked her what happened. It was a question with no answer.

A woman named Helen was having dinner with me one time. She kept saying over and over that she did not know how she got to Aston Gardens, but she planned on finding the answer to the puzzle. She told me she was living in a house in Sun City Center, making the house payments and taking care of things. Then she was surprised to find herself living in an apartment in Aston Gardens. She claimed someone chose the living quarters for her, and she could not figure out who did it. I finally asked her if her children could have put her here and she said, "No, they live in Pennsylvania and I don't see them very often". I suggested she go to the front desk and ask the desk clerk that question. Somehow I began to feel she would not bring her problem to the front desk, and maybe the mix-up was in her head.

I had dinner with a woman I like to call the "grape lady". She would always ask her server to bring her a fruit cup, but take out all the fruit except the grapes. One server asked the dining room manager, if she could do this and was told no. But I noticed she got her bowl of grapes anyway. I also noticed when I asked for the fruit cup that there were usually only a very few grapes included. Oh well!!! I do love pineapple!

One resident couple was so friendly and the husband told jokes every time I would eat with them. How he could remember all those jokes was a mystery to me. One day he brought a folded piece of paper to the dining room and wanted to show me how the results of his cutting would end up as "Hell"—specifically a Nazi Swastika and a cross. He must have gotten mixed up in the folding or cutting as it did not work out. I finally told him I did not believe in Hell and I needed to return to my apartment and my cat.

One night I had dinner with Nona and her caregiver. She tried to stay alert for the dinner conversation, but I could see it was hard for her. She would tell me wrong information and her caregiver would correct her—over and over. Then she said she could no longer talk—over and over. The truth was she could not remember what she wanted to say and her caregiver could not read her mind. I learned later she would be moving to Pennsylvania to be near her daughter soon.

I sat with a woman one evening who used to be an interior decorator and had been married to a man who managed an Ethan Allen store. She was very frail but always dressed stylishly, wore lots of silver and turquoise jewelry and played bridge on a regular basis. Sadly, a few months later there was a red rose in the lobby and the announcement of her death.

I was seated one night with a woman who used very few words. The conversation and my questions went like this: "What building are you in?" She said, "#2". I then told her I was in building #8 and her comment was, "Oh!". Then I asked her where she was from and her short reply was, "Philadelphia". I told her I had lived in nearby Haddonfield at one time, and she said, "Oh!". Then I asked a final question, "Do you have children?" and she responded, "Three, living". Her only other words were, "I hear there is to be a root beer float party". I wanted to just reply, "Oh!", but I did make a longer comment—then we sat in silence.

I met a nice couple one day in the dining room who had been married for seventy years. He was ninety-four and she was ninety-two. He told me he walked three miles every day. Amazing! I made a mental note to attend exercise class that next day.

Kathy was my dining companion quite a few times. When I first met her she seemed very tired and not very interesting. Then she told me she had just finished kidney dialysis. She explained she had to go three times a week for the rest of her life. This got my attention. After that I warmed up to her as even under that aura of fatigue she evidenced she was a very nice person. I was ashamed of myself for thinking her uninteresting. First impressions are often wrong.

I arrived at the dining room one night and a walker was parked just outside the entrance. It had a cap sitting on the seat that said, "World War II Hancock, Kamikaze Survivor". I remembered that my husband was on his destroyer that went to the aid of the carrier Hancock when it was hit by a Japanese plane. Many men were blown into the water and Gordon swam to the disabled ship to rescue several men in that bloody, shark-infested ocean. I found the owner of the cap eating in the dining room with his wife and we talked about the incident and arranged to meet in my apartment later where we exchanged stories, books and photos. I even showed him my Gordon's war diary where he related his story of the disaster. It turned out that we both lived in the same building—just down the hall from each other.

I had dinner with Martha and listened to her interesting stories about her nursing career. We also found out we both liked real life murder stories and trials, so had that in common. She told me she wanted to write a book about Aston Gardens, nursing, or some other subject, but felt she was not qualified. I recognized the way I felt about writing years ago, so encouraged her and told her I felt she would indeed be a good writer as she had such a need to tell. Her attitude changed with my encouragement and she said she would start a book—soon.

One day as I was having my dinner alone, the servers, the

head of the dining room and the assistant chef were all frantically checking under tables, chairs and in all the corners. We heard later they were looking for an unnamed resident's dentures. I don't know if the teeth were ever found!

A woman formerly from Europe agreed to join me at my table. She did not seem to like the American way of doing things and wanted to be viewed as very European. We spoke of our travels and I felt we had an interesting conversation about many things. So after we were done with our dessert and coffee I said to her, "I have thoroughly enjoyed eating with you, but I must return to my apartment." Her demeanor changed and she said, "Are you going to leave before I am finished?" I told her I thought she was done, and I sat meekly in my chair while she had two last sips of her apple juice. Then she put her glass down, saying, "Now I am done", and stood up and left.

I was asked by the sales representative at Aston Gardens to have dinner with a prospective tenant named Rosa. She was ninety-one years old, had no kids, lost her husband six years before, and had published several books. After a pleasant dinner we went to play bingo in the Ballroom. I won the first three games and Rosa won the big prize of $22. Somehow I felt the other players would be happy for us. Then why were they looking at me as if they hated me? Maybe it could be because they had been sitting for hours each bingo night studying their cards and hoping to win. Then a newcomer like me comes in and takes three prizes and another woman who was not even a resident comes in and wins the big prize. That was my last bingo game for several years, not because of this treatment, but I just found other things to do.

One night I watched Dr. Phil on the television and then hurried down to get to the dining room about 6 p.m. (It closes at 6:30 p.m.) in time to get the food selections I liked. A woman named Gladys asked if I wanted to sit with her for dinner. She assembled several diners who were alone and let them sit at a table for six with her. They each had interesting stories to tell of their past. You never know what confessions or stories you will hear from your dining companions.

On Memorial Day 2015 I was asked by a neighbor, to eat at their table set for seven. I noticed that everyone at our table were residents who had been here for a long time and were all here when I first came in 2005. I sat beside Marge who was one of the original residents from way back in 1999. Soon we were trading stories of the old days and one of the most interesting was told by one of the men at our table.. He said Aston Gardens held an outside picnic in Veterans Park on another Memorial Day over ten years before. It was a hot, hot day. The tent and tables were all set up and soon the delicious food and residents arrived and the fun began. The only problem was that the area was infested with fire ants. Between the painful fire ant stings and the swarm of flies, it was a very short picnic.

At a later date, I sat with Marge and listened to some good stories of her early days at Aston Gardens. First, she told me she was ninety-eight years old, which makes her one of the oldest residents at Aston. Then she told me that when she moved into her apartment building, the builders had put a glass door on the bathroom in the foyer of her building. No one wanted to use that bathroom for any purpose, with so much exposure. I wonder why they had to change it to a solid door!

Marge also told me about how three majestic sandhill cranes made three holes in her porch screen when the neighbor's bird feeder ran out of food. She loved to see these cranes and hear their raucous cry when they flew overhead.

Sometimes I would sit alone at a small dining room table and just watched the residents come by my table. The man we know as "Colonel" with his Air Force cap, Paul with his positive attitude, Mike and his "care giver" who not only smiles when he meets anyone, but always gives the lady a kiss on the hand, and Marion who seems to be searching for someone or something—maybe her past—are just a few of the ones who made a lasting impression on me. The food is always good, but it is the residents who make this time of day special.

RESIDENTS TO REMEMBER

CHAPTER 5

Some of the most interesting humans who entered the portals of Aston Gardens are included in the following accounts. Everyone in Aston Gardens has fascinating stories to tell about their past, career, or travels. I chose my "Most Interesting Resident List" for a variety of reasons. To respect privacy I have not used the resident's real names.

THE FLYING RESIDENT

This gentleman who was so involved in all aspects of flying was probably the most interesting resident I found during both my stays at Aston Gardens. He was born on a farm in New Brunswick, Canada. He attended a one-room school when farm life permitted. When he was fifteen his family relocated to the United States in 1930. Due to the depression he could not attend college so he worked for the railroad and saved enough money to enroll in an aviation school in New Jersey. He learned how to repair airplanes, got an aircraft mechanics license, and also received his special flight training, although he was mostly self-taught.

Following the bombing of Pearl Harbor, he accepted a commission in the U. S. Marines and after three years of training he was sent to the Pacific. After the atom bomb was dropped he returned to his hometown and established a Flight School. He later became an aviation inspector for an insurance company and moved to Florida.

He was a part of the "Greatest Generation", but I believe his most interesting accomplishment was the building of "Miss Emile", his own homemade airplane. A friend told him one day, "You have to build an airplane." He responded, "No way!". But after enjoying two flights across Canada in his friend's homemade plane and considering the fact he needed a distraction while caring for his wife, Emily, who had Alzheimer Disease, he placed an order for an identical kit to the one his friend put together and began working on "Miss Emile".

This man wondered how he would build an airplane in his garage and still watch his wife who needed attention almost twenty-four hours a day as an Alzheimer patient. To his surprise she was content to watch him and numerous helpers work, especially when their two grandsons, Andrew and Jeffrey, were there. The boys were ten and twelve years old when the project was started, and later learned to fly the airplane they helped build. This project was therapy for Emily and our avid flyer and a real learning experience for the grandsons.

As the project progressed he wanted to attach the wings to the plane in his driveway. A member of the local Experimental Aircraft Association agreed with his wish and said, "Go ahead; then we will move it to the airport." After tolerant neighbors had endured strange noises for two years they were prepared for anything. Not so for unsuspecting drivers who came close to several mailboxes as they stared in disbelief at this plane going down the road.

To transport an airplane down Route 1, the Sheriff Department required a permit, and Sunday was the date they chose. At 6 a.m. Sunday morning the unusual procession rolled down the highway. Miss Emilie was escorted by two sheriff vehicles with flashing lights, followed by five cars loaded with helpers who had picked up this 1,010 pound airplane and placed it on the truck. The fourteen mile journey ended at the airport and all went well.

This well known flyer wrote many articles for *What's Up* after he became a resident at Aston Gardens. One article entitled, "Air Ambulance Flight", described how it was forty years ago. The co-pilot's seat would have to be removed in this small plane so the stretcher could be strapped in. The pilot had to climb over the stretcher. One of the flight students was a local doctor who elected to fly most of his seriously injured patients to better equipped hospitals within a three hundred mile radius. The doctor pilot needed easy access to the patient so he could administer a hypodermic needle to handle the pain. Many of the flights were at night so faith in the engines was often tested.

The Flying Resident passed away April 20, 2010 at the age of ninety-three. I must say, he certainly lived a very full life.

Ice Hockey Champ

The most famous resident who ever moved into Aston Gardens was an interesting man of ice hockey fame. John became important in my life as we had a romance for several years. While I was working on the Welcome Committee I was asked to go downstairs in my building and greet a new resident, and take him to the dining room for his first official dinner at Aston Gardens.

I had done my homework and read all about John in *What's Up* and various articles they had included to introduce him to the residents in Aston Gardens. He grew up in Medford Massachusetts where he spent his young life ice skating on nearby ponds. He graduated from Medford High where he was Captain of his hockey team and excelled in that sport. This sportsman was good in baseball and football, but it was ice hockey where he gained his greatest notoriety.

In 1948 he attended the Olympic Games in St. Moritz, Switzerland where his team won the Bronze Medal. From 1949 to 1951 he was a hockey star at Boston University. He played in the National Championships and was All American for two years and led the country in scoring and was later inducted into Boston University Hall of Fame, and later into the National Hall of Fame. He was known as Boston University's greatest player. Whenever this champion laced up his ice skates he dazzled his fans with his high scoring heroics.

After college he taught history and coached throughout his career. He also coached baseball and basketball. He was a hockey official for many years and created the first ice hockey scoreboard. Two semi-professional hockey teams, The Collegians and The Eastern Olympics were started by this man. He operated and coached many youth hockey camps and clinics. He served in the Armed Forces in World War II.

This special man was married to his beautiful wife and helpmate, for over sixty years. They had five sons and one daughter. His sons all played ice hockey in various colleges.

This interesting family all flew to Africa and drove across the continent in a Volkswagen van from Morocco to South Africa, camping all the way. They hosted over two hundred students in their home so the young people could study at nearby colleges.

During that first evening together John and I talked about our African adventures and began to get to know each other. He asked me to attend the New Year's Dance with him a few nights later and I agreed. This began a relationship that lasted for several years. We went to dinner most nights together. On Friday nights a musician, Ed, came with his keyboard to play the old songs for us old people in the lounge and we loved to go and sing along. We both knew the words to most of the songs that were played, like, "Yesterday, When I was Young" or "Night and Day".

Sadly, my hockey boyfriend was afflicted with Parkinson's disease. He either refused to let it limit his dancing or his body was so strong from the years of hockey that he could exert lots of energy. We danced to romantic music like, "September Song" and "Dancing With Tears in My Eyes". It was wonderful, and I felt so alive again. When he took me back to my apartment that first New Year's Eve we kissed as a way of beginning our late-in-life romance.

Slowly my friend developed some dementia, but even this only caused distractions in his life. One night he had a problem with his memory and on the way to dinner he seemed agitated and unsteady. Finally, he said, "My wife is gone and I can't find her." I did not know what to do so I tried to reassure him that everything would soon be alright. We sat on the couch in the foyer of the Clubhouse and I asked him who he thought I was. He told me he felt I was his best friend. I excused myself and went to the desk and quietly asked the desk clerk to call his son who lived in Tampa. Soon his son arrived and he told his father that his mother had died and calmed him down. Then the three of us had dinner together and all was well again.

This amazing man usually walked with a brisk, steady gate, exercised daily on the walking trail near the Clubhouse in Veterans Park, swam with me in the pool, and played golf. As a couple we became news on the Aston Gardens gossip-line, an active group who covered everything from romances to who spilled soup on their clothes and had to wear a bib.

Eventually I had to stop the fast dances with my partner due to my heart problem, so when the entertainer played the fast dances I would lend him to an eagerly awaiting group of women with the promise they would return him to me when the next slow dance was played.

Our relationship was over when I moved out of Aston Gardens to buy a house with granddaughter Windy, and this hockey champ moved to Orlando to be near his son who was transferred there. Later he went back to New England to be near the rest of his family as the dementia progressed. I called now and then, but he was unsure who I was. The last time I talked to his family they told me he was resting, so I told them that when he got up, if he remembered me, he was to call. He never called again.

THE TRAVEL AGENT AND THE PILOT

This former travel agent and pilot friend are a familiar couple around Aston Gardens. The pilot would often be seen carrying a cup of morning coffee to the travel agent if she were not feeling well. They both had apartments in my building. When I was here the first time I enjoyed seeing this couple arranging fresh flowers for each dining room table each week. The two of them were editors of *What's Up*. Both were very active in Aston Gardens life and did a lot of volunteer work to be helpful.

The Travel Agent grew up in Michigan. She married another Michiganite and they had a son and daughter. Her husband was in the military and she operated four travel agencies and was in charge of many tour groups. There was a lot of industry in that area of Michigan and she arranged travel for many of them. When she retired they came to Sun City Center and bought a house. After her husband died in 1992, this travel agent moved to Aston Gardens in 2003.

Our former pilot was born in Cedar Rapids, Iowa. He was married for the first time for twenty-eight years and his second marriage for thirty-five years. He was a World War II veteran and served as a pilot who taught instrumental flying in Waco, Texas. He accumulated a total of 1800 hours of flying time.

MISSION NOT IMPOSSIBLE

This resident was born in New York City and his wife in Endicott, New York. He was a Certified Public Accountant and Vice President of the New York City Stock Exchange. Then they both volunteered for seventeen years as active fund raisers for the Mission Aviation Fellowship. They were flown in single-engine airplanes to remote areas and jungles in Africa, Indonesia, Australia and Europe to learn what was needed for the money the mission raised.

THE LIVABOARDS

This Livaboard couple were two of the first people I met when I moved into Aston Gardens in 2005. I was attracted to them when I heard they had lived on a boat for many years. My husband and I lived on an old yacht, the Rubaiyat, for a few years, and they were probably the best years of our lives.

The captain was born in Sayre, Pennsylvania and the first mate in Yonkers, New York. He was president of a company that made primary flight instruments for all major airlines. He later owned some small water treatment businesses. It was after selling those businesses that they decided to live on a boat. Nine years ago they moved ashore to Palm Coast, a town half way between St. Augustine and Daytona Beach, Florida. It was the fastest growing town in the United States at that time. Later they moved to Aston Gardens.

THE LITTLE ITALIAN DRESSMAKER

This Italian dressmaker was born in Italy and moved to New York in 1955. She became a dressmaker in New York City and made gowns for movie stars for twenty-one years. She was married for fifty-one years and they had a son and daughter.

She moved to Aston Gardens in 2008. She loved to dance, listen to music and sing with her great Italian operatic voice. Often she would sing loudly in the dining room and some of the residents would groan, but I loved to hear her.

AIRLIFT CHARLIE

Charlie was born in Patterson, New Jersey. He was married for fifty-six years but a widower for five years when he came to Aston Gardens. He was a pilot with the 15th Air Force during World War II, flying B-24's. Charlie participated in the Berlin Air Lift in 1949, but did not stop flying until 1990 even though he retired from the Air Force and worked for the National Cash Register Company. When he came to Aston Gardens he played a lot of golf and looked forward to learning how to dance.

THE WORLD TRAVELERS

This world traveling couple became Aston Garden residents in 2006. They had been married for fifty-eight years at that time. He was born in Cheshire, England, she in Wales. He served in the Royal Navy in World War II going to the Mediterranean, Indian and Pacific Oceans. He met his future wife after his discharge in March of 1945 and they were married December 26, 1946 on Boxing Day in the United Kingdom. They left England in 1948 for Sydney, Australia where he joined the Goodyear Tire and Rubber Company, a firm with twenty-five factories worldwide. He stayed with them for thirty-five years until retirement.

After seventeen years in Sydney, they moved to New Delhi, India to work with International Goodyear. After New Delhi they moved to Casablanca, Morocco which was a French-speaking country. Before going there the company sent this interesting couple to Berlitz for a six-month French course. After Casablanca, He was transferred to Africa and worked there eight years as a CEO.

When Goodyear was informed of his decision to retire and live in the United States, they said that if he would stay there for one more year that they would do all that was necessary in assisting this couple in getting Green Cards, which in those days was no easy matter. When they were told the process would take about a year, he told Goodyear he did not want to sit at a desk in Akron during this waiting period. Goodyear suggested that they could visit factories around the world and make a report on various aspects of the experience. This was a wonderful opportunity to see old friends again and go to new places. So starting off in Australia they worked their way gradually north and west, visiting many countries. Finally while working in Rome almost a year, they were informed that the Green Cards had been approved. Soon they were officially American Citizens living at Aston Gardens.

A TOUCH OF INDIA

A very special lady moved to Aston Gardens in 2008. She was born in India but had been a United States citizen for twenty years. She was a librarian in her younger days. Her beautiful family visits here on special occasions. I must say, just looking at her is a positive experience. She always has a smile, kind words and is loved by everyone

MANHATTAN MOTOR SCOOTER

This motor scooting mama always rode a motor scooter in her room, down the halls, in the bar and dining room. She often drove it to the birthday parties and then sat wistfully watching the dancers enjoy what she could not. She always attended cocktail hour at the bar each evening before dinner and would imbibe two or more manhattans each time she was there. Then she would order another one or two manhattans to ride with her to the dining room. After dinner she would stop by the kitchen before heading back to her apartment to get some food treats for her dog, Tony, a Yorki. Tony actually had "Meals on Wheels".

I learned more about this lady's way of life when I substituted for my granddaughter, Windy, who often took care of and did odd jobs for this lady. My routine that was that I went down from 4:30 to 5 p.m. taking her a tostado from the kitchen for her snack on Sunday evening, since we only had one meal on that day. While there I got her pills to take with the can of beer she needed to have with her tostado. Then I walked Tony. I had been informed that Tony pooped twice a day, so I could only concentrate on the "peeing". Tony would walk out into the yard, get his peeing done and then sit down. No amount of begging, cajoling or ordering could move that little dog until I would head for the door going back to the apartment where he lived. Then about 9 p.m. I returned to walk Tony again and make sure she got into bed safely without falling. She would ride her motor scooter into the bedroom and bathroom and then transfer to a walker to take the last few steps to the bed. I would assure her that Rosie, her usual caregiver, or Windy would be back in the morning, and then I would turn off the lights and leave.

Several years later I found she had moved to Palm Gardens as a nursing home type patient. She remembered me and seemed resigned to her fate, but I knew she missed her manhattans and especially her little dog, Tony.

THE ASTRONAUT

Bob was born in Kalamazoo, Michigan. He married in 1941 but had been a widower since 1975 when he entered Aston Gardens. He attended the Notre Dame Graduate School as an aero-space engineer. Bob trained with the original seven astronauts and participated in the program putting Neal Armstrong on the moon when he worked with the original shuttle in Houston, Texas.

STINKY

Mary moved into an apartment in Aston Gardens, at the other end of the hall from my apartment, in 2006. She was born in Ohio, married in 1939 to a chemical engineer who was involved in the space program. Mary was a former teacher and a stay-at-home Mom when her children were small. After coming to Aston Gardens she got involved in bridge. She was ninety-four years old. We became friends and it was so much fun to be with her at first. Then I began to realize there were times she was displaying confusion and forgetfulness. It was hard to socialize with someone with these problems.

Mary often referred to herself as "Stinky" (for good reason). When she played bridge for the first time with me, she wet her pants and did not want to get up and leave, as everyone would know what she did. I kept urging her to go and promised to walk behind her to hide the wet spot. Finally we departed for our apartments.

I answered the phone one morning and she told me there were three women in her apartment and they left, and she did not know where they went. She said one of them slept with her, but left the next morning probably because she snored. I asked her if she knew the women and she said they were her granddaughters. Later in the same day when I talked to her she said one of the women was her daughter.

One night when we had dinner together she ordered her meal and then forgot she ordered it. She even stopped a waitress to ask if she had taken the spaghetti and meatballs to the wrong table.

One of the most upsetting episodes I had with Mary was when she rang my doorbell at 1 a.m. one morning. She told me the flood waters were rising (we are on the second floor) and she heard women near her room talking about it, and a man with a flashlight was shining it on the creeping water, and she was frightened. What was I to do? I was standing there in my nightie and no teeth! So I told her she was just dreaming and in reality there was no high water or rain outside. I put in my teeth, dressed in my robe and walked her back to her apartment.

Slowly things got worse. Mary would get angry with me for letting her sit for hours at the elevator in our building while I tried to call her from the Clubhouse as I waited for her there. Then after she apologized for her anger we agreed to have dinner together. I had to go over and get her. She just seemed to remember nothing that was said. I decided to slow up my friendship with her as it was upsetting too much of my life, but I did not want to just drop her as her need for a friend was great.

Then the next problem came up at the last dinner we had together. She seemed very upset and told me she was missing some very valuable jewelry. I wondered at the time if this would come back to haunt me as her daughter had given me the key to Mary's apartment in case she needed me to go in and check on her when the phone did not work. I gave it back that very day. I knew that her daughter may have taken the jewelry out of concern for her mother's changing behavior and then Mary forgot that, or she may have put the jewelry in a special hiding place and then forgot where she put it. We never knew for sure.

Eventually Mary moved to be near her daughter and get more family care. In spite of all the problems here, she did not want to leave.

I tell this sad tale about Mary because she was part of my experiences in Aston Gardens. Some residents have the beginning of dementia when they move in and it slowly worsens. When they need more assistance or are unsafe to be alone, then they either go into Assisted Living or move near their family, as Mary did at the end.

DANCING DAME

This dancing dame was the editor of *What's Up*, the monthly newsletter about Aston Gardens. In the early years *What's Up* was a source of so much information for my book on Aston Gardens; the history, the residents and the politics. I still remember her dancing so expertly in the ballroom at the resident birthday parties. She always sat at the same table closest to the dance floor with a select few joining her there.

Just a bit about this active resident, she was from Massachusetts and graduated from Pittsfield High School. She took post-graduate courses until she was eighteen and then got a job with Berkshire Life Insurance Company. She loved reading, dancing, ice skating and walking.

She married her first husband, John, in 1941 and had two daughters and one son. John was a World War II veteran who served with the Jolly Rogers in New Guinea and flew fifty-eight missions there. He died in 1978. She then married Philip and they worked as dance teachers in the Academy of Ballroom Dance for twelve years. This lady then came to Aston Gardens and contributed so much to all the lives here.

MEANT FOR EACH OTHER

Ray and Olivia were both born in Allentown, Pennsylvania and attended the same elementary school and high school where they graduated in 1936. Then they lost track of each other for fifty-five years. Ray was a Naval Carrier pilot and lived many different places in the world. Olivia worked as an auditor for Coca Cola in Bethlehem, Pennsylvania. Each married different people on the same day, May 25, 1940. Both Ray and Olivia lost their spouses to death and met each other again at a class reunion in 1992 and got married in October of that year. You will probably agree they were meant to be together.

THE HAT LADY

The hat lady was born in Portland, Oregon. The family moved to Minneapolis, Minnesota when she was six years of age after they lost everything in the depression. She met her husband in high school and they were married in 1946. He was a pilot stationed at the Miami Airport. They had six daughters and one son. The first child was born in Pago Pago, American Samoa, just after World War II. Her husband met

General Chenault in an airport in Honolulu and they started the first airline in China called the Civil Air Transport.

This traveling lady had a very interesting life. She got a degree from the University of Minnesota and spent many years as a pain clinic worker. She arrived in Sun City Center in 1992 and became Ms Sun City Center in 2000, crowned by the Classica Club. She taught for six years in the United Community College and volunteered with the Emergency Squad here in Sun City Center. She spent part of her time at Aston Gardens writing a book about her life. Probably she will be remembered the most for her collection of fifty hats. She will always be known as the "Hat Lady".

MY NEIGHBOR

My neighbors moved into Aston Gardens in the fall of 2005. They had been married for sixty-two years. He graduated from Massachusetts Institute of Technology and she from Wheaton. This attractive couple met in their college days. Both of them liked to square dance, play golf, tennis and bridge. For thirty-seven years they had lived in Towanda, Pennsylvania where they raised their four children. She was a 'stay at home mom', which I believe to be the hardest job in the world.

He was employed by Sylvania Electric, later taken over by General Telephone and then by Verizon.

I knew this special couple when I was first at Aston Gardens, and when I returned in 2014 I lived right across the hall from her, so it was nice to be near someone familiar. Sadly, he had passed away just before I arrived on the scene. By now, she was in her mid-ninety's, still driving, walking briskly, and still so friendly. She never complains and feels so lucky to be here as she now has few worries and responsibilities and a chance to just enjoy life.

A NICE GUY

Mr. Nice Guy is not a resident but he does transport residents to and from the Clubhouse, works as Security Guard, is the weekend movie operator—and so much more. He has a laugh that makes you love life, a relentless urge to be of help to residents, and the way he walks makes me want to get going and do things. All this can be summed up with the words, "Nice Guy".

THOUGHTS OF AN OLD WOMAN

CHAPTER 6

As I sit in my apartment in Aston Gardens daydreaming of the past years, I like to think of the wonderful memories of my youth. We did not have Ipads, tablets, cell phones, computers or even televisions, so our time was spent playing hide and seek at dusk, hopscotch on the sidewalks, ring around the rosie or London Bridge. We jumped rope, climbed trees, bounced up and down on the bed (a great trampoline). I remember running through the sprinklers in the lawn with such pleasure, and even taking a refreshing swig of water from the hose. We made the drink of summer, Kool Aid, or got refreshing ice cream treats from the Good Humor Man (I can still hear that jingle of his truck). Cereal boxes and Cracker Jack boxes had amusing prizes in the bottom. What fun we had!!!

One of my favorite things to remember was catching fire flies in jars and then using the lights from the jar to read a little more after our parents called, "Lights out" at bedtime. I loved to hear the sound of crickets and other night noises. In fact, in later years when I was diagnosed with Tinnitus, when the ringing in my ears was so annoying, I tried to pretend it was just the cricket sounds again.

I remember my first day of school and how scared I was. Christmas mornings were always exciting. I recall my first crush and first kiss. The boy who kissed me was gentle and exciting.

We talked a different language then they do today and never spoke in initials. "Sounds like a broken record" is out-of-date today as there are no more records in use. "We were in like Flynn" is passé, as Errol is long gone. I am not sure who Riley was, but "Living the life of Riley" is no longer used. "Kilroy was here" was said, but he is not here any longer. No one now says, "Heavens to Betsy", "Gee Whillikers", "Jumpin Jehoshaphat, or "Holy Moley". The word "swell" is not used. It went out with pageboys, knickers, poodle skirts, saddle shoes, Mickey Mouse watches, hula hoops, skate keys and candy cigarettes. "Hubba-hubba", go necking, petting, smooching, spooning, billing and cooing or pitching woo are so out-dated. So is "See ya later, alligator". I hear your answer from the shadows of time, "After while Crocodile."

A saying I always loved was, "Life is not measured by the number of breaths we take, but by the moments that take our breath away". In my life the breathless moments included the following: Being made snow queen at school when I was young—Skylark, my horse when we lived on a farm—my first plane ride to St. Croix on Pan American Airlines—Cocoa, my horse in St. Croix—Gordon getting the Bronze Star Medal in World War II for saving lives—Gordon coming home from the war—our wedding—the births of our three children—our first television—Gordon graduating from the University of Maryland—Europe on $5 a day—going to the Bahamas twice on our boat, the Rubaiyat, while living aboard—Karen graduating from nursing school and honoring me with a poem—realizing Stephen, my grandson, would live after his diving accident—publishing my first article in the magazine Golden Years—our 50th Wedding Anniversary trip to Greece, Egypt and Tanzania, a balloon ride in Tanzania, and a camel ride in Egypt—recovering from malaria and possible death—Windy drug free at last—and many more.

Now I am in the winter of my life and I am living in a strangely different world than I knew as a young person. Now so much more can be said or shown on the television or in movies then in the days when Rhett Butler's "I don't give a damn" shocked the country. Kids now play violent games on computers or video games which gives them the idea that killing someone is exciting and acceptable. Sex is now allowed on the media making viewers "horny" so some of those who used to keep their desires in check now act out in violent ways. There seem to be so many more suicides, murders, rapes and molestations.

Maybe if I tell a few things I believed in, lived by, aimed for, or was helped by, it would give some of the younger generation some help in facing their own old age years. Looking back on my life I think about some of the aims that brought me satisfaction like hard work which gave me such a sense of accomplishment, a feeling of pride and an independent spirit. Children should be told that life goes by so fast. They should enjoy what they can, but must plan ahead for a career and the future. Marriage, the old fashioned way, gave me stability and brought meaning to my life. All relationships take work, patience, understanding and lots of love. I can't say enough about love being the most important part of every life. Live your life fully, follow your dreams when you can, and enjoy the ride. Laughter is so important, but the most important thing is love.

I tried to stay flexible all through my life, especially in old age as I have known so many old people who were so set in their ways and they missed out on so much enjoyment in life.

I believed in God and the power of prayer, but cared little for organized religion. I believed in living my beliefs as much as possible. For most of my life the outdoors and wilderness were my church. I always loved the natural settings, wild animals and birds.

I gathered a few sayings I want to share with you to help you on your own journey:

"Aspire to inspire before you expire."

"The things you used to care to do, you no longer care to do, but you really do care that you don't care to do them anymore".

"Frustration is trying to find your glasses without your glasses."

"The irony of life is that by the time you're old enough to know your way around, you're not going anywhere."

"I was always taught to respect my elders, but it keeps getting harder to find one!"

"It is better to walk alone, than with a crowd going in the wrong direction."

"Do not regret growing older as it is a privilege denied to many."

"Going out is good, but coming home is better."

Old age brought many changes. My interests changed with my ability to do things as I aged. I used to love walking in the woods and climbing mountains, but now the walks must be very short or "none at all". I had to give up panning for gold and rock hunting, but now I can only write about it all.

I did not anticipate memory would be such a problem as I aged. You can read lots of books, study in school, attend cultural events, but you need memory to enjoy or use your experiences later in life. The problem with short-term memory loss in my "old age" affected my conversations and even telling funny jokes as I would forget the punch line. People you are talking to find it hard to follow what you are saying if you keep stopping to try to remember a fact or a name.

When I was young I did not understand why health was such a constant topic of conversation between older people, but I know now. In the older years, each day brings new pains and aches and conditions affecting the body. I had to learn to deal with or solve the health problems, but constant talking about them was so boring to me and others. So I seldom did that.

I used to see old people bent over, slowly walking along—and I made up my mind to never let myself get that way. Now I realize some elders can't help how they get around if they have had a stroke, Parkinson Disease or other crippling diseases.

When I was younger there were often pictures of old people slowly rocking in a rocking chair. In today's world the older ones are often exercising, off to classes to improve the mind or volunteering for some special needs group.

I remember reading, "The most important things in life aren't things". As I look around my apartment I see the furniture I bought so long ago. It all has a use in my life for sitting or sleeping, but I feel no deep emotion when I look at or use it. I do not love it. That emotion is reserved for people, or my special friend, Tory, the cat. When I am gone the furniture will probably go to the Salvation Army for someone else to use. Even my jewelry is just an adornment on an arm or neck that has dark spots and more and more wrinkles. I wonder at times why I want to draw attention to my aging skin.

Speaking of changes in life's journey, the biggest change made all over the world is what we do with our elderly. In the past civilization we often moved the aging person into the homes of family members for care. Anthropologists unearthed the bones of an early human who lived approximately 500,000 years ago. Analysis showed the bones belonged to an aged and disabled man who would have had trouble walking or carrying the slightest load. To live this long despite his disabilities he must have had support from others in his group. This shows that senior care is at least a half million years old and that caring and empathy are core human traits.

Governments eventually began to provide income to older people when they could no longer work. In 1935 Social Security was passed in the United States under Franklin Roosevelt. In 1965 Medicare and Medicaid were formed giving more seniors access to getting medical care no matter what their means. This change alone opened up the doors to Independent Living complexes like Aston Gardens and more people could afford the extended care of such places. *1

If you are not in the winter of your life yet—let me

remind you it will be here faster than you think. We are so unprepared for the last phase of our life. I believe I am in the right place at the right time in my long life—Aston Gardens, my home.

*1 (From A. Hesberg of Caring For Our Elders by Jeff Anderson.)
Copyright 2014 A Place For Mom, Inc. All rights reserve

EPILOGUE

This is my story and my book concerning my life, so I wanted to tell my readers about the end of my life, how I feel about it, and how I will face it when the time comes. It is not depressing—just part of life.

My heart doctor found I had a damaged heart valve and a decision must be made as to what to do about a situation that would eventually end my life. Should I go through with open heart surgery, should I try the most recent and less invasive procedure of going up a vein in each leg, meeting in the heart where the surgeon can repair the valve, or should I do nothing?

The procedure going up the veins would not prolong my life, but could give me better quality of life. The doctor gave me many tests of the heart to be considered in any decision, and told me what he felt I should do. He said I was ten years too old (I am 89) for open heart surgery, so the risks would be too great. He felt the other procedure was too new and had too many side effects (one was stroke), so he did not advise doing that. He felt I had four to five years left before the heart gave out and said I should not do anything but just wait. I had a dilemma to sort out. I would ask others including my family but it would be me to make the final decision.

I never expected to live to be 89, so to make it to 93 would be a gift. I decided to do nothing and enjoy a few more years. I have time to get everything in order before I depart. Many people don't have that chance. I hope to be mentally alert to the end, I do not fear dying, and will be ready when the time comes.

Aston Gardens is the right place for me to spend my last days!

BIBLIOGRAPHY

1 (From A. Hesberg of Caring For Our Elders by Jeff Anderson.)
Copyright 2014 A Place For Mom, Inc. All rights reserved.

ALSO BY BARBARA

Letom, Motel Spelled Backwards
The True Story of a Mom and Pop

Follow in His Footsteps, The adventures of my father

Come Fill the Cup, A true story of a livaboard

Sea Cove Cooks, Recipes from Motel guests